HOW TO
LEAD YOURSELF:
THE ROAD TO LEADERSHIP

Tatianna Pavlidis, Varun Potlapalli,
Rishi Parikh, Nehali Watwe, Catherine Cobb

Limits of Liability and Disclaimer of Warranty
The author and publisher shall not be liable for your misuse of this material. This book is strictly for informational and educational purposes.

Warning – Disclaimer
The purpose of this book is to educate and entertain. The author and/or publisher do not guarantee that anyone following these techniques, suggestions, tips, ideas, or strategies will become successful. The author and/or publisher shall have neither liability nor responsibility to anyone with respect to any loss or damage caused, or alleged to be caused, directly or indirectly by the information contained in this book.

The 1/1/1 Leader Project

Sign. Set. Smile. Serve. Spread. Share. Simple.

One for yourself. One for someone else. One for the community.

http://www.divyaparekh.com/111-leader-project/

FOREWORD

Having worked with Divya over several projects and counting her as not only a colleague but a friend and leadership coach, it is no surprise to me that she has inspired these young authors to pursue their dreams in entrepreneurship, leadership, and kindness. Her ability to encourage others to succeed is what makes her such a successful coach, speaker, and teacher.

The Leadership Project and Entrepreneurship Program that these young authors write about are essential in today's global marketplace. As they share their experiences, readers can see how each teen used the skills learned in these workshops to improve their lives, overcome obstacles, and shape their middle school and high school years in order to thrive in a competitive job market. Add to that the kindness and high standards of ethics each young author uses to enhance his or her life, and you can see the recipe for their success can be the recipe for your success too!

The book is designed to reach out to the younger generation(s) to cultivate positive change and ensuring that the up-and- coming adults of tomorrow have a valuable skill set that will improve their own lives and the lives of those whom they encounter. Readers will learn valuable leadership skills, which is high in demand given the global marketplace, and will also learn how to overcome obstacles, such as bullying. Additionally, readers will find inspiration to become better citizens, leaving the world a much better place.

Finally, by introducing the world to the 1/1/1 Leadership Challenge, the book takes the leadership and, kindness to the next level and encouraging everyone to do so as well. Because with compassion, we create connections, and after all, connections are the most valuable resource we have.

I hope you all will enjoy this inspirational work as much as I did and may it encourage you to be the change you wish to see.

Jessica Cory
Lecturer in English at
Western Carolina University

ACKNOWLEDGEMENT

Thank you to everyone who made this book possible. Most of all, thanks to Coach Divya for not only bringing the team together, but pushing us to be our best and giving us invaluable life skills from day one.

DEDICATION

To all the young leaders out there, and the
unlocked potential waiting within.

ABOUT THE AUTHORS

Tatianna Pavlidis has been writing ever since sixth grade, from stories to books! She is a freshman in high school, living in North Carolina. "How to Lead Yourself" is the first book that has been published. Tatianna is very passionate about sports, her family, and helping others. Throughout the book, she has showed great signs of maturity and motivation. During middle school, she was the captain of the soccer team, faced many obstacles, and learned a lot about herself. Tatianna has been a great member to the "Fabulous Five."

Varun Potlapalli is a 14 year old high school student that loves to write. He is ded icated to helping himself grow as a person and become more actively involved within his community. His first novel, for which he is a co-author of, is "How to Lead Yourself." The reason he is writing this is because he is very passionate about becoming a leader and helping his society grow. He has had thorough leadership coaching, and he is well-educated about the world around him.

Rishi Romil Parikh, the President of the 1/1/1 Leader Project, has been raising awareness to create kinder communities for the younger generation. In this book, Rishi aims to further educate the new generation on the power of kindness and magnify compassion one person at a time. Rishi employs leadership skills in everyday life

and events, such as group work, robotics, and mentoring. Rishi enjoys guitar, basketball, and learning about engineering in his free time. Rishi is a rising high school sophomore in North Carolina.

Nehali Watwe has enjoyed journaling throughout her life. She is a rising high school junior from North Carolina. Nehali has done multiple leadership workshops with Coach Divya and has worked closely with the 1/1/1 Leader Project and its application in personal, educational and professional settings. The leadership principles she's learned have since become a way of life for her. She is currently a fellow with a presidential campaign organization and working as a leadership mentor with young children. Along with enjoying spending time with family and friends, she is passionate about dancing, reading, and playing basketball.

Catherine Cobb has loved writing since before she ca n remember. As a high school senior in North Carolina, she's participated in every class from Advanced Literature to Creative Writing, and has also served as editor for the yearbook, writing captions and editing copy while designing typography and layouts. She's participating in leadership coaching with the DP Group and is excited to extend what she's learned to others around her. Although she's interested in writing, her true passions extend to science and design. Her goals for the future are bringing together the arts of engineering and communication to better the world around her.

CONTENTS

INTRODUCTION

What has happened to communication? No, not texting or social media, but human connection. The structure of communication amongst people as we know has collapsed. Today is the era of experimentation where the connectivity and convenience of social media and internet connected devices have replaced direct communication between people. The primacy of trust in any relationship is just as important today as it was when George Washington was alive. People have to make extra effort to build trust in today's society, as it is easier for people to claim they are something they are not behind the curtain of social media.

Then one might ask, what would happen if we brought back authentic communication? The possibilities for the greater good would be endless if we taught the younger generations how to lead their way into creating a kind, compassionate, and collaborative community in which they lived. This is where the 1/1/1 Leader Project comes into play. The 1/1/1 Leader Project is a simple goal setting plan that brings one closer to their community and builds them as an individual. The 1/1/1 Leader Project consists of four simple steps: First, sign the pledge and commit to the completion of the project. Next, set a goal for yourself. It can be anything, from keeping your room clean, to working out every day. The next step is to smile. Make a commitment to smile to at least one person each day. It's a small gift, but it can turn someone's day around. Finally, do a kind act for someone. Keep it simple, like holding a door open for a person behind you, or picking up trash around your neighborhood. Through these small acts, you can help yourself and your community improve for the better. Helping friends, family, and neighbors get started with the 1/1/1 Leader Project can help make a larger ripple in the community. In order to do something big, we need to start small with everyday acts that lay the foundations of trust and communication between people.

When I was teaching undergraduate and graduate students as an associate professor, I would see kids who had the desire to excel fail because they could not afford tuition. They would work two jobs to pay tuition and they wouldn't have any time to study. I wanted to help them, so I offered to tutor them for free. Their grades went up to A's and B's and they went from I can't, to I can, to I did. This fueled my desire to help students. Even though I have primarily coached entrepreneurs, leaders, and achievers, I have made it my business to ignite the passion of leadership in our younger generations as they will be leading the community of tomorrow.

When getting the authors of this book together, we had one end goal in mind. We wanted to share a message of leadership with today's youth so they learn to lead themselves and become the humble and strong leaders of tomorrow. The stories these kids share in the book are there to inspire the rest of their generation to take lead of their own destiny, embrace challenge with courage, continue to improve, be kind and create a better community.

Throughout the book you will find various elements of the 1/1/1 Leader Project. The project helps people get on the right track to a better society and a better self. The journey of the authors and how they have come together to form a team and work for a common cause to contribute to the community will surely help motivate you to start the 1/1/1 Leader Project yourself.

Become the author of your own life and write your story positively—be happy giving smiles to someone and form connections through kindness. Bring awareness to society that helping others and giving back to the community is an integral part of life.

Don't forget, receiving begins with giving.

Hugs and hearts,
Coach Divya

1

Perserverance

"I can't change the direction of the wind, but I can adjust my sails to always reach my destination"

—Jimmy Dean

In the summer of 2013, I, Tatianna, enrolled in a summer leadership program. I was entering the sixth grade, and being my first year in middle school, I was very quiet. Not only that, but I was shy, and not confident. My family and I moved a lot, so making friends was always difficult for me. When my mom told me that I was going to a camp to learn leadership skills and become more confident, I was worried because this wasn't how I hoped my summer would start off. All I could think of was what the camp was going to be like. I was hesitant about the camp, and didn't know what to expect.

Since the fourth grade, I always had a fear about being left out and ignored. However, once I walked into camp, my fear suddenly vanished. For once, I felt like this was where I wanted to be. I was so used to being behind people's shadows and having people take advantage of me. Often, when walking into school, I would have the feeling that people were judging or making fun of me. But when I walked into the camp, I experienced such a welcoming feeling from Coach Divya. I knew I that had never experienced this sensation anywhere else.

During the first couple of days, I noticed that not everyone was comfortable yet. The energy in the room was very low. Coach Divya and Rishi both encouraged all of us to become leaders, and to support one another. However, as the environment made us more comfortable with each other, we wouldn't stop talking over each other. Rishi and I got to know each other better and that helped me become more comfortable. Since Rishi helped facilitate previous workshops, he was very relaxed and helped the other students and I feel at ease.

Throughout camp, I made quite a few friends. One who stands out is Skylar. She is very outgoing, and that's what helped me have an immediate connection with her. During the camp, Skylar taught me that there is no reason for fear to exist. Fear is something that holds you back from your full potential. A leader leads one's self and others.

As camp progressed, we did all sorts of activities. For example, we had a leader lead us around the room while doing fun, and sometimes even embarrassing, actions. Every participant got the chance to be the leader.

When we walked up and down the rows doing embarrassing actions, at first I was uneasy and very timid. As I became more comfortable, I thought about doing an embarrassing action. Nonetheless, the feeling of being judged by others came back. Like I said earlier, as the camp continued on, I became more comfortable with the people I was with and eventually faced my fears. I did that by doing an embarrassing action that everyone did with me. What motivated me into doing the embarrassing action was how everyone else was not shy. They didn't care about what others were thinking; they just laughed and enjoyed the moment. Rishi was very helpful in this workshop because he was instrumental in putting us all at ease. It was incredible to watch myself go from being diffident to having tons of fun!

Coach Divya made the camp very enjoyable yet very challenging at the same time. She pushed us to become better people and helped us reach the goal we each made at the beginning of camp. The camp was about a week long, and towards the end of the week, each of us had to prepare a small presentation about what leadership really meant to us. For me, leadership doesn't have a true definition. Instead, leadership is a goal that people want and continue to work toward every day. You have to be able to lead others with positivity and encouragement through your actions. I took home from the camp that you can't be who your friends want you to be. You have to be someone you're not scared to be. Not only that, but you can't allow other people to dictate your life. You are the leader of your life, and no one can change that. Not only did the camp give us an opportunity to become leaders, but it also gave us the chance to help each other grow.

The most memorable moment I experienced at this camp was on the very last day. Coach Divya asked us to raise our hands if we would be interested in taking another step towards being a leader, and be part of the 1-1-1 Leader Project. Surprisingly, everyone raised their hands. It was a great feeling to experience, because it showed that all of us were willing to change our lifestyles and become leaders. The 1-1-1 Leader Project is where you give, receive, and spread kindness. It all starts with one good deed. With that one deed you can change a person, which could one day transform the whole world.

The Before and the After

Before the camp, I was very confident in myself, however that didn't last very long. I knew who I was, but I changed myself for my friends. I changed who I was because I had more trust in my friends than I had in myself. My friends had always taken advantage of me, which wasn't the greatest feeling. Some days after school, I remember being so upset and hurt by who my friends were and started to cry. Coming home from school crying wasn't the life I wanted to live. Because of the camp, I regained my confidence and felt I could take on different goals in life. It was time to take action! From that day forward, I wanted to put a stop to all the things that brought me down in life. If you can't lead yourself, then how can you lead others? In my room, I have a board that is filled with all my goals and hopes for life.

> Number 1 - Go to College
> Number 2 - Get Good Grades in School
> Number 3 - Be Patient with my Family
> Number 4 - Gain a Better Relationship with God
> Number 5 - Have an Impact on Someone's Life

These goals helped me to be focus on the moment and to relax. Yes, many of my goals take place in the future, but one goal that I could work on immediately was number five: have an impact on someone's life.

How to Make It Happen

I was about six years old when I found my role model. She was in college, but yet she found time to babysit my brother and I in the summer. She was everything I wanted to be in life. From the moment I met Mikayla, I knew I wanted to be like her when I grew up. She was many things, but the characteristics that stood out to me was how she was smart, confident, loyal, strong-willed, and was very strong in her faith. Mikayla was very inspiring because she had set goals in life and reached all of them. Reaching goals that you set in life is the best feeling a leader can experience. After meeting Mikayla, I told myself, "This is what I'm going to be one day." I thought that at the time it was possible, but as I got older I realized that it wasn't that easy to be the person you one day hoped to be. It was time to put a stop to everything that was making my life miserable. I started taking baby steps. However, the first step was coming out of my shell and doing something I never imagined myself doing. Going to the leadership program, I knew, would help me to face my fears. The dreams I had for myself would one day become a reality.

After the camp, Coach Divya and I met once every two weeks to discuss things that were happening in my life. We also talked about how I could positively affect the people around me. She had given me homework one session, and it was to do an appreciation activity with my family. But what's that? An appreciation activity is when one family member is supposed to write one nice thing about all of the other family members. This would rotate and there would be a new member writing nice things every week. Coach Divya assigned me multiple activities to help me just relax and appreciate the things I have been blessed with. During the summer, when the breeze is nice and the sun is glistening in your hair, Coach Divya and I went on nature walks. We walked in different directions every time. On our walks, we would stop and hear the trains passing by. If we didn't hear trains, we would stop to hear the pinecones falling to the ground from the trees. Nature walks really helped calm me and put me in a relaxed state.

Leadership Experiences

Being young, there are several different ways you are able to display your leadership skills. Leadership can be shown in many other ways than just books. One way could be through sports. I have a deep passion for soccer.

I have been playing it ever since I was in kindergarten. It was the year 2014, and soccer season was right around the corner. Trying to get placed onto a team is hard, but trying to become captain is even harder. Being captain isn't based off skill, age, or experience. Instead, it is based off your ability to encourage and motivate your teammates. After long practices of training and motivating others, it was time to vote on who would be captain. I had worked hard trying to become the captain. But I didn't do it just for the title. I wanted to be captain because I knew I had the chance to inspire and bring out the best in others. Ever since I was a little girl, I always had the desire to have an effect and an impact on people's lives. It was the night of the vote and I was anxious to find out who was going be the captain. At practice the next day, our coach announced that I was going to be the captain. I heard everyone screaming and congratulating me. That was a significant moment I will never forget. I told myself later that night that I didn't want that feeling to ever go away. I wanted to keep succeeding and being proud of myself and what I have accomplished.

Since Coach Divya trusted me, and I believed in her, I knew I could be a great captain. She told me that I had what it took to take on the task, and I knew she was right. When I told her the news, Coach Divya and I celebrated by running in the middle of the street and dancing. During the middle of our season, our soccer coach was going through a hard time and started to take it out on us. It was halftime at one of our games and he decided to get up and leave. He had walked over to the baseball fields and just started talking to the coach. Being a captain, it was my responsibility to keep the team motivated. After a pep talk, the team was ready to go and win! That day I believed that I could not only lead myself, but I could lead my team. From that season, I learned that if things are not going right in your personal life, you have to still consider others around you. The point of being a leader is to guide yourself and others in times of need.

It was the summer of 2015. We had just got out of school and I was so ready to have the best summer ever. A few weeks after school ended, my family and I went down to Myrtle Beach to start off the summer.

It was all fun and games, but then the summer took a wrong turn. I hit my head hard. I became lightheaded and dizzy. This was the last thing I expected to happen. When we got home, we went to the doctors and they said I had a concussion. They instructed me to rest my brain, which seemed almost impossible. But the worst part was having no engagement in physical activity! This part was the worst because I was planning to attend the NC State Soccer Camp with my old soccer team from Ohio. It was supposed to be like old times, but you can't always get what you want. At first, I was really upset and at that moment, depressed. I was scared that I was never going to be the same. Worrying, being scared, and having fears are not traits that a leader is supposed to have. However, I soon realized that this experience was exactly what I needed. I needed to know that I was going to be okay, and to lift myself up. I was not only going to be okay, I was going to be better than I was before. This officially became a comeback!

Having a concussion set me back in my leadership work. I remember having a meeting with Coach Divya and my mother. Coach Divya asked me a simple math question, and I couldn't answer it. Instead, I just burst into tears. At that moment, I felt that I let everyone down, from myself, to my mother, to Coach Divya. Letting people down is one of my biggest fears in life. However, that day made me realize that I needed to pick myself up from a mistake that I made and start over. After that day, I worked on my leadership and math skills every day. Session after session, I started to feel better. I felt rejuvenated and I started to see the light out of my dark days. The summer was unfortunately over, but it was the best summer I've ever experienced! This was because I was determined and motivated to become the leader I wanted to be. Let's just say that my comeback was successful.

Time Management

Being a teenager, your life revolves around social media and what your friends are up to. At least that's what I thought. My life used to be all about my friends. But slowly, as I got older, I realized that I was blocking everything that was important to me in life. I had a wall that separated me from my family, school, sports, and most importantly, God. I was not proud of who I used to be. Friends used to be everything in my life. I used to spend about two to three hours a day face-timing and/or chatting with my friends. At that time in my life, I struggled in school and didn't seem to care. I had to learn how to say no to my friends. When you are in times of help, you just need to stop, think, and reprioritize. Making a list can help you manage and prioritize your time wisely. For me, when I prioritize, it helps to use a calendar. I include all the tasks that I have due either that week or for the month. Using a calendar helps to manage time efficiently and it also gives you a perspective of what the month is going to look like, so you can work ahead, instead of cramming homework or projects the night before.

For example, in school your schedule looks like this:

1st Period - Math
2nd Period – Science
3rd Period – English
4th Period - P.E/Health
5th Period - Lunch
6th Period - History
7th Period - Spanish
8th Period - College Preparation

If you had a math test, history homework, and an English paper all due in the same day, which one would you do first? Well let's break it down.

1. Always start with the subject or homework that is due first. After you do the subjects that are due first, next you work on the tasks due later on in the week.

2.   When prioritizing, it is important to do things that are easier and then work yourself towards the things that are harder and need more time.

See? It is just two simple steps! So now, if you had a math test, (which you need more time to work on), history homework (which is easy for you), and an English paper (which you need a lot of time to work on) all due in the same day, which one would you do first?

First, you would do your history homework, since it is the easiest one and will probably not take a lot of time. Secondly, you would study for your math test because it will be a little harder to study for. Lastly, you would do your English paper, because it will definitely take more time than your history homework and studying for your math test.

Leadership in Action

Leadership is a long-lasting process. As for me, what's next? In the future, I plan to be a team captain for a walk that is helping raise money and awareness for the Too Much T.V. (TMT) Youth Community Foundation. In preparation for the walk, I plan to raise four-hundred dollars. I plan to teach the kids in the program how to manage their time and how to manage their future businesses. For this phase, my co-authors and I have all worked together to make flyers and bring awareness to everyone around us regarding the program. We have all dedicated our time to one another and to helping these children.

My three take away points:

- To achieve goals in life, you have to believe in yourself. Believing in yourself is the hardest thing about being a leader because you may have set many goals in life and fall short of them. However, you have to learn that the mistakes you have made and the goals you have fallen short of are what makes you who you are. You just have to pick yourself up, and apply everything you have learned from falling short, in your everyday life.

- Standing up for yourself is a sign of confidence. Standing up for yourself is being able to say no and still being who you are around other people. You have to be confident in who you are because you can't allow other people to dictate your life. Each of us has been given a unique life that we should live up to. Standing up for yourself is just one way you can live the way you want to. I have learned that we don't need to change ourselves to help others.
- Time, time, time! Every day, we lose time, and it never comes back. Prioritizing may seem like a short-term effect, but I promise you it helps in the future; that's why it is good to manage your time wisely by prioritizing.

2

From Determination to Success

"A leader is one who knows the way, goes the way, and shows the way."

—John C. Maxwell

When I, Varun, was 8 years old, the Chinmaya Organization for Rural Development (CORD), which was an organization dedicated to helping destitute people in India, demonstrated to me what leaders were. I learned that leaders are not only found in workplaces, or are not just elected officials, but are also found in day-to-day life, as they help other people become successful by achieving some sort of goal or standard and by helping themselves to develop as leaders in the process. The principle of CORD is also the main goal of Habitat for Humanity in the sense that they both strive to help people who need it. I was fascinated at how many people around the world dedicated their lives by building basic necessities to help people who were facing hard times.

From that point on, serving the community became one of my goals; leading myself and others to help those who were going through hard times. I searched for opportunities from then on, and I found a workshop that was run by Coach Divya. This was an Entrepreneurship and Leadership Workshop that taught kids how to become entrepreneurial leaders in their community. This workshop clearly defined for me what a leader was, as I learned that being a leader is not just for helping the community, it is for helping yourself as well.

Leadership: What is it?

The dictionary definition of leadership is the power or ability to lead other people, a group, or organization to achieve a goal. However, my take on this dictionary definition is when someone motivates a group of people to achieve a certain goal, all while growing as a person him/herself.

I have become a more driven leader in my community because of this definition, so that I can learn more about myself and the people in my community. I get an "eye-opener" every time I volunteer because I discover new things about myself. I am now more closely involved with people in my community through these "eye-openers" and am more inclined to helping them.

What I Learned from My Role Models

I have been inspired by leaders of the Chinmaya Balavihar who volunteer to educate young kids on how to live their lives, act as role models to them, and give the youth spiritual insight on the way of life. These leaders are always open to ideas, and are always willing to lead their students to their goals. They listen to their students' problems, and provide methods to solutions, all without "spoon-feeding" them the answers. At the same time, these leaders are also able to get the students to reflect on themselves and who they are, and this ability is fascinating to me. One example of this ability that fascinated me was when a teacher was able to get the most talkative student to introspect on himself with amazing logic. The teacher had filled up one jar with beans, and left another jar almost devoid of beans. Our instructor then told him, showing us the filled jar, that one with lots of knowledge did not make as much noise (which meant talkativeness). Our teacher shook the jar, and unsurprisingly, the jar made no noise due to there being no space to make noise. The teacher then told him, showing us the mostly empty jar that one with little knowledge made lots of noise, and shook the jar. The jar, due to there being lots of space for the beans to move, made a lot of noise. This example impacted the student very much, and from then on, he was one of the biggest contributors to class discussions, and he was one of the most insightful students in the school.

Additionally, the goals that the students want to achieve are achieved with the help of the leaders; the willingness of the leaders to listen to their students' problems is astounding and remarkable. For example, a student was stressing out about an exam that was coming up, and the teacher did not have an answer for her because the teacher was facing the same problem with a project deadline coming up at her workplace. However, they collaborated and were able to think the situation through, providing a very interesting and efficient solution, which was breaking time up into work/study sessions and reserving time for free time, because they both knew that just "not procrastinating" wouldn't work. This taught me an additional lesson about leaders, in that they do not have to know every-thing; they can grow as people as well.

The type of leadership that the Balavihar leaders demonstrated really stood out to me, and I made sure to incorporate them into my life, into middle school, and my day-to-day life.

A lesson that I learned in Balavihar that I was able to incorporate into my real life was not using "harsh" or "bad" words. Before Balavihar taught me, I was always unsure why I couldn't use "curse" words, even though I never used them. I always hated being told not to do things without being told why. The teachers at Balavihar explained to me that the words were "bad" because they were defined that way by society, and that others would take offense to it, even if they were just words. They told me that "if people took offense, it would hurt your reputation and that they would not listen to you ever again, and when you tried to make a good point, they would not listen". This thinking allowed me to finally realize why saying the harsh words were bad, and so I never used them.

I used the characteristics of leadership that I witnessed at Balavihar in my Taekwondo assisting experience. I was part of a Taekwondo Honors Group, which helped younger students learn martial arts. I taught them how to perform everything they needed to know and the leadership I had learned in Balavihar was largely responsible for my ability.

This leadership also allowed me to grow in the process. I specifi-cally remember one instance in which a student would not listen to me while I was teaching him a critical move for passing a Taekwondo test. The student was using a different move, which he thought was right. The instructor, who was senior to me by 5 degrees, came over to check what was happening. As it turned out, the student had been right, and if I had used my technique at testing, I would have failed and the younger student had passed. I had learned a lot about myself, realizing that I had much to work on as a Taekwondo student and a leader. In addition, I also learned that knowledge can come from anywhere, which was a lesson about humility. Overall, using the leadership techniques that Balavihar had taught me were extremely helpful for teaching these younger students, and helping me learn more about myself.

For Myself, Young Students, and my Community

I am writing this for two reasons. One reason is to educate and instruct the younger version of myself who wanted to start the leadership journey.

When I was younger, I wanted to be a leader but I had no idea of how I could give back to the community. In addition, I was lost as to who I really was with the changes associated with middle school such as peer pressure, fitting in, and communicating with my peers and staff members at the school. I was learning to be a leader, and it was a tough and long journey. It was a great struggle for me to become a leader, and the qualities of leadership were not easy to learn.

There were plenty of aspects to work on such as being able to communicate with people and their families, being able to help no matter the situation, and being able to incorporate leadership in daily life. There were many road bumps on the way, and the path was not an easy one. There were many difficult tests to become a leader, and these tests took a while. The path to leadership is a journey, and the means to completing the journey is the most rewarding.

The second reason I am writing this is to help my community. There is a huge community of charities, friends, and family that I am involved with, and this large community could use leaders to help those in society who need it. I have helped a lot with organizations in my community, such as the Salvation Army, the Morrisville Youth Leadership Council, Habitat for Humanity, etc. and these experiences are what has motivated me more and more to become a productive member and leader in my community. I feel that I need to help my community, and I will do whatever it takes to accomplish this.

My Story

I started out as one of the people who needed to achieve a significant status in my social world. I was not exactly sure how to reach my goal, and I was lost in my community. I soon found out about an opportunity when I was 10 years old about a camp being held for entrepreneurs by Coach Divya. I attended her camp and it was there that I felt I could do something significant in the community and develop myself as a leader at the same time. I felt this way because it was a chance for me to finally explore what being a leader was all about, and it was a chance for me to find out how giving back to the community and developing myself worked.

Even though there was the regular stress of middle school, I still felt confident, even though at times I felt uncertain because it was the unknown that was scary to me. After this camp, I did not volunteer much, and I lost touch with volunteering and leadership. However, an opportunity to display what I had learned in the camp, which was leadership, arose in my Taekwondo class. In addition to assisting the younger students with their martial arts, part of becoming a black belt was doing a community service project. I knew this was my chance to try and make an impact on the community and develop myself as a leader and discover new things about myself, so I decided on doing a Coat Drive to the Salvation Army. I was deeply touched when we dropped the coats off because as my family and I walked into the Salvation Army Headquarters, a woman asked for a coat for her little baby. It was so heartwarming to know how much a little action could help so many people.

However, after this event, I lost touch once more with the community around me, and with the burden of middle school, I got busy with increasing responsibilities, such as studies and chores. Later in my life, at the age of 12, I joined a new Leadership Council, this one for Morrisville. It was officially called the Morrisville Youth Leadership Council, and I realized I had to join and rise to a high position in the Council in order to use my leadership skills once more. We in MYLC held car washes, and I was emotionally touched when the money we raised for a boy who was dying was used to help prolong his life.

After joining MYLC, I looked for more opportunities. At the age of 14, I found out about Coach Divya's leadership group, which had criteria for acceptance that included kids who really wanted to impact their new communities and give back to them, while developing themselves as leaders. These kids also wanted to become active leaders in their society, and I felt this was a perfect opportunity for me. The people chosen for this group were handpicked by Coach Divya herself. I was able to get in.

There were many struggles with the group and volunteering; however, in the end, we were able to overcome them. One example was how we had to take a group picture for this book. Coach Divya had to take a picture of three of us (Rishi, Catherine, and I) but the picture was coming out terrible. We desperately tried to take another picture in the same room, but the picture would not come out right. We had to problem solve in this situation, and we came up with the idea that we could take the picture outside in nature. This brilliant thinking and logical problem-solving was a part of what I learned with Coach Divya.

With Coach Divya, we also volunteered at the Wade Edwards Learning Lab with the Too-Much TV (TMT) program. We volunteered at a camp and I learned more about teaching younger kids, especially more stubborn ones who did not want to be there. I learned that to help those types of kids, I had to make the subject appealing to them, not necessarily directly out of the curriculum.

I also learned through the group with Coach Divya, how much of a sacrifice people were making to write their chapters for this book. I was one of those people because I was about to go on vacation before this book was published, so I had to work extra hard to make sure that my part of the book got done. This experience taught me that one must do whatever is necessary to complete the task in front of him/her. I learned with Coach Divya that one can do a lot in a little time if one really puts his/her mind to it, puts their emotions, and puts the "right" work into it.

How I Met People in the Leadership Group

When I joined Coach Divya's leadership group, I had to meet many new people. These were other leaders in my community who were experienced and more educated in the ways of being a leader than I was. The knowledge I learned was put to the test when I had to work with these leaders. I realized that when I became a leader, I chose to involve myself with other leaders in my society, and the whole community at large. I was being put on the same level as them, and I had to learn quickly the ways of the world of leadership.

It was a difficult transition into this social world. However, thanks to Coach Divya's guidance, I signed up for the 1/1/1 Project, which was a pledge to do good acts. This was a step closer to my transformation as a leader. This transformation is very important to becoming a great leader and a well-respected person because of the character development that was involved with this change. I, along with Coach Divya's group, started going and reaching out to the community in many ways. We volunteered at camps in the Wade Edwards Learning Lab, and this experience taught me much, such as a deeper level of being a leader, where one has to take the initiative to develop themselves.

My Three Key Messages

Through my experience as a leader, I have composed three key messages for younger kids who want to become leaders. These three key messages, in the end, are what were able to make me a leader of the community today.

One message is to never lose motivation. It is extremely hard to regain motivation after it is lost. Motivation is the force that drives someone to become what they are, in this case, a leader.

The second message is that one must be willing to help others. Being a leader means to help others as well as helping yourself. However, when helping others, one must not just do it for themselves; they must do it for themselves and the community.

The third key piece to becoming a leader is to be resilient. Being resilient means to be able to bounce back when tough times hit. When one decides to traverse the path to becoming a leader, there will be some tough times. Being able to come back and remain an effective leader in the process is what defines someone as a leader.

The Conclusion

In conclusion, a leader is someone who takes on responsibilities to improve themselves by giving back to the community. They take on these responsibilities through their own initiative, and this initiative is a motivation for them to help their community more. The person who wants to become a leader must be willing to take the steps to becoming one, and must tread the path required.

I have learned many things as a leader in my community. I have learned that leadership is, on a certain level, the same as serving the community. This is because being a leader is partly defined as someone who helps the community through service and, in the process, helps develop himself/herself. From my experience with the Salvation Army, with the lady asking for a coat for her baby, I was able to realize that being a leader is not just about being able to lead a group of people, but it is also about serving the community at the same time.

Another thing I learned as a leader in my community was how serving the community makes one grow. When someone serves the community, the individual realizes and understands the world around him/her better. Interaction with others is required when serving the community, and getting to know other figures in society is very critical to a person's development. Human beings are social creatures, so meeting new people and becoming involved with the society around us is crucial to being a better person.

I have had a lot of experiences in my life while becoming a leader, many trials, many paths to cross, and many "eye-openers." Some of these experiences are thanks to Balavihar, Taekwondo, MYLC, the Salvation Army, and Coach Divya.

I am currently developing and am on my path to becoming a leader in my community. I know that it is not an easy one, but with Coach Divya's help, I will become able to achieve such status. I plan to continue with Coach Divya and her team to reach out more to the community and we are looking forward to doing even more.

3

Setting a Course for Leadership

"Being a leader is about becoming
independently confident, responsible and inspiring others
to do the same as you build your circle of influence. Leadership is
about being your best, doing your best and bringing your
best to your personal life, professional life and every
situation you come across."

—Rishi Parikh

Mr. Richard and Mr. Sonny were two of the most influential and import-ant characters in my life. It all began on my first day of kindergarten when I, Rishi, excitedly ran onto the bus without look back to start the biggest adventure of my life. Of course, my mom always reminds me of how independent I was from such a young age. After boarding the bus, I met one of the kindest people I would ever meet in my school system – my bus driver, Mr. Richard. Every morning he would smile at me, and it would always give me a positive outlook on the rest of the day. Also, whenever the older kids would bully me and the younger kids, Mr. Richard would step in and stop their bullying. Due to his involvement, the older kids left us alone. He would always give me great advice about good study habits, how to make friends, and was always there for me and my friends. I did not realize how much I looked forward to seeing Mr. Richard every day until we got a new bus driver in second grade. I realized that I carried happy memories and lessons I learned from Mr. Richard, as I was reflecting upon who had impacted my life.

Mr. Sonny was the crossing guard at my elementary school. It did not matter whether the weather was cold, hot, rainy, or sunny, Mr. Sonny would always show up to his job. What set Mr. Sonny apart from the other employees was that he would show up with spirit. Mr. Sonny never stopped smiling, and would always wave to everyone. He would always be kind when helping kids across the street. Mr. Sonny's positivity impacted me, as he soon became my role model. Mr. Sonny showed me that you can bring leadership to your job and to others no matter who you are and where you are. I was always excited to wave to him, and I would ask my mom to bring him warm coffee on cold wintery days. The kindness he exuded created an impact and was an inspiration to the entire school. Even in middle school, we would drive past my elementary school, and I would be put in great spirits when I would see Mr. Sonny smiling. Unfortunately, Mr. Sonny died in December of 2015, and he has been dearly missed.

In second grade, most of my friends had started playing the piano. My mom had asked me if I wanted to play piano as well, but I did not want to do what the majority of the other kids were doing, so I told my mom I wanted to play guitar. I needed to take lessons, and even though I was only seven years old, my mom put the task of finding a guitar teacher in my hands. One of my neighbors played guitar, and I approached him one evening to ask him if he could teach me. He said no after explaining he did not have enough time. I idolized Patrick and wanted to learn guitar from him. I stood there and asked politely once again if I could learn from him. He looked at me, smiled, agreed to teach me, and I started taking lessons every week. Each time I would go, I would walk down my driveway, look both ways on the road multiple times, and then I would take confident strides to his house across the street with my guitar strapped to my back. I learned to follow through until I reached my goal; however, I did not completely embrace guitar. Due to school and my extracurricular activities, I had stopped playing guitar, and it started collecting dust in my attic.

One of the extracurricular activities I was doing was Tae Kwon Do, which is a form of martial arts. In elementary school, I was bullied and teased, and I was determined to put a stop to that. Tae Kwon Do helped me stand up for myself and gave me a lot more self-confidence. The school I went to for Tae Kwon Do did multiple outreaches that I was a part of, and one of them was to my elementary school. We demonstrated breaking boards and self-defense maneuvers, and the kids that saw me demonstrate stopped teasing and bullying me. In the rare case that someone would try to bully me after that, I would square up my shoulders and look them in the eye and tell them to stop. This helped to build the confidence I have as a leader.

One day in fourth grade, Coach Divya (my mom) was approached by a classroom teacher who told her that I was a well-behaved kid who connects with other students, similarly to how well the teachers noticed her connecting with students when she would come to volunteer. The teacher then asked if Coach Divya would be able to do a leadership club for some of the students who were emotionally challenged and doing poorly in class. Coach Divya enthusiastically agreed to do so. As we set the wheels in motion, Coach Divya received the list of students she would be running the leadership club for. Coach Divya noted that some of the kids were struggling with ADHD and Asperger's syndrome. Like all people have moments of doubt, I saw Coach Divya hesitate. Coach Divya told me that although she was a trained and certified leadership coach, she was not sure if she would be able to make a real difference in these kids' lives. I believed in what Coach Divya could do, and after reassuring her that she could do it, I volunteered to assist in the leadership workshop. Coach Divya and I started waking up earlier than usual before school twice a week to arrive on time so we could set up the leadership workshop. On the first day, I asked Coach Divya if I could lead the workshop, and she was delighted at the idea. In order to get to know one another, Coach Divya asked all the kids why they joined. Most of them said that their parents told them they had to go and others stated that their video games would be taken away if they did not go. As we got to know each other on the first day, the kids shared how they felt about themselves and the world – angry, upset, hopeless, and disappointed.

As the leadership workshop continued, I eagerly participated, doing whatever I could to make the kids feel at home and part of a team. We grew together, and they became enthusiastic to come early to the workshop as well as participate in the critical thinking exercises. As we progressed, Coach Divya asked the kids once more why they were coming to the workshop. The kids said they were coming for themselves because they felt proud of themselves and enjoyed coming to the workshop to learn. Not only did the kids increase their emotional resilience, but their grades began to improve. So many times when I would see my friends smiling and answering with enthusiasm, I felt joy. From this began what is now known as the 1/1/1 Leader Project.

Coach Divya and I had worked together to create the 1/1/1 Leader Project. To create a better community, we created a pledge, which anyone can sign on Coach Divya's website. The pledge is a contract requiring the signer to do three things: 1) Give at least one smile every day to someone to make their day 2) Do one small act of kindness every day, and 3) Set a goal, no matter how big or small, to achieve for her/himself.

We live in a world that becomes more connected every second, or so they say. Technology helps us contact friends and family from far away, and technology helps us reach others more quickly. Developments in the economy help us move money and investments, while the increase in technology is building up our global brain. With all these advancements, our most important framework is the global heart. Not only has the global heart been diminishing, but society has become more judgmental and less sincere. Etiquette is falling through the cracks in our perception of a better community. Society is a road in need of paving, and the 1/1/1 Leader Project is here to pave our social structure and build a community of connected and helpful people.

Early in fourth grade Coach Divya introduced me to a concept I did not think I would use for the rest of my life. It was introduced to me through an interesting old folklore:

> "There was a queen who had six princesses. When the queen was on her deathbed, the royal council staged a competition to elect their next queen. On the day of the contest, the council men and women waited for the princesses to come and show their talent. The first princess came, Princess Sight, and by her power, she created amazing images that captured everyone's attention. Princess Smell came next, and by her power, created intense and powerful aromas of flowers and perfumes that made everyone relaxed. Then came Princess Taste, who waved her magic wand and allowed the audience to experience the flavors of the most delicious food. All the council men and women murmured among each other, thinking that Princess Taste should win. Princess Hearing stood up confidently and created beautiful music that filled

everyone with emotions. Princess Touch created love and harmony, and at the end of her performance had everyone hugging those that they loved. All the five beautiful princesses looked at each other, thinking that they would be queen. The royal council was in a dilemma, as they did not know who to pick. The royal council was debating the merits of each of the princesses when the sixth princess, Princess Breath, who was rather plain in looks, came along and said that she was the one who deserved to be the queen of the kingdom. The royal council asked her what she could do with her power, as she had not shown them anything yet. Princess Breath told everyone to focus on breathing in and out. The council men, council women, and other princesses ignored her, thinking that Princess Breath was ordinary because her power was something they did every day. They dismissed her as a potential queen of the kingdom. The queen had asked Princess Breath to promise her that she would stand up for herself when they were electing the next heir of the kingdom. Princess Breath thought that she had kept her promise to her mother and decided to walk away. As Princess Breath walked away from the princesses, the council men and women, every-one began to gasp for air. That's when they all realized Princess Breath's importance. After understanding her true power, Princess Breath was elected as queen of the kingdom. Princess Breath said if we work in uni-son, the power would be stronger than if she ruled alone, and that's how the technique of the fist focus came about."

The concept taught to me was about both calming down and realizing inner strength through an exercise that involves making the hand into a fist. To perform this, you make your hand into a fist by closing your fingers one at a time while taking deep breaths each time until your hand turns into a fist. As you monitor your breath, you calm down, and when all your fingers are together, you can see that you can have strength as a team in the same way your fingers can be strong together, like a fist.

As I progressed through elementary school, I was able to build up my leadership skills, and being part of the AIG (Academically Intellectually Gifted) program improved my odds to go to clubs that build confidence and leadership. Clubs I attended in elementary school were the Koalaty News Network (our school's mascot was a koala), the Safety Patrol, and Peer Tutoring.

The Koalaty News Network (KNN) helped me build confidence because I had to go in front of the camera in front of the entire school. This improved my confidence when talking to others because what I did was aired around the school. KNN also taught me responsibility, as I had deadlines for researching information to use on air. It took me a while to get used to putting myself out there on camera and learning to meet deadlines, but once I did, I was able to use these skills as a foundation for what I gained in the upcoming years.

In fifth grade, I volunteered to help the second graders out in academics. As part of what we called the Peer Tutor program, I gave one-on-one tutoring lessons to a fellow second grader. Helping him with math, I was able to guide him through everything he did not understand. As we worked together, he looked up to me in a way that made me always think of how I could best help him. This helped me become outgoing and friendly and expressed my love of helping others.

In fifth grade, I also joined the Safety Patrol club. My job was to work alongside four other kids to help kids safely get out of their cars before school and into their cars after school, along with opening car doors for the kids. One day, a cool two-door car pulled up to school (the Toyota FJ Cruiser). All of us were fighting over who would get to open the doors, and I decided to take this situation into my hands. I first got everyone calm and asked who wanted to open the door. Since all five of us wanted to open the door, I proposed that we could take turns and get a chance once a week. Many similar incidents arose when I was in the Safety Patrol club which taught me how to lead and manage a team. These skills became especially useful during group projects in the following school years.

The year I was transitioning from elementary school to middle school, I had many choices of where to go. The majority of my friends from elementary school were going to our neighborhood school, West Cary, or a magnet school, Carnage, in Raleigh. There was one other choice for me: Ligon Magnet Middle. I knew of no one going there; however, it had exceptional academics. Unlike Carnage, it was not accepting more than its student capacity and had over 200 electives. Even though I wanted to be with my friends from elementary school, I decided to apply to Ligon. I learned to become independent, as I was able to make new friends and excel in my academics. I got all A's in my first year of Ligon. I was able to lead myself instead of following others to a school which could be the wrong fit for me. In Ligon, I was able to experience many clubs and electives which I could not in my neighborhood school, and I was able to meet new people who were very talented and friendly.

I enjoyed making an impact and helping other kids when I had assisted Coach Divya in elementary school. When Coach Divya began summer workshops, I decided to come along and help while participating. In every workshop, I saw some kids who were extremely exuberant and participated in everything, and some kids who would listen and try to remain in the shadows of others. As a participant in one of the workshops, I volunteered to be a member of the group that did not participate much. I would slowly create opportunities for these kids to talk to make the workshop a comfortable space for them to speak what was on their mind. Tatianna, whose chapter you may have read earlier in the book, was in our leadership workshop, and she did not speak a lot initially. As I helped Coach Divya form the groups, we paired Tatianna with a confident and helpful girl. To help break the ice at the beginning of the workshop, we did something we called circle time. In circle time, we would share with the group something that was good about our partner. We would try out a different icebreaker every day to accommodate different personalities. Since several participants liked soccer, we decided to play soccer; however, we were not allowed to talk during the game, we were only allowed to talk before the game and in timeouts. The purpose of this was to help strengthen our communication skills. Tatianna was a great soccer player, and this activity sparked her enthusiasm and helped her become comfortable in the workshop.

Halfway through middle school, a friend of mine had decided to start a robotics team with four other kids and myself. Since none of us had access to an ample workspace, we joined a group which is now called The Forge Downtown. As part of The Forge Downtown, we got access to tools and opportunities for outreach. Due to the nature of our robotics league, FIRST Tech Challenge, outreaches and "Gracious Professionalism" were encouraged. Gracious Professionalism is defined as helping your opponent be at their best when you compete; and in a way, required leadership. We would step up to help other teams when they were in need of assistance and parts. Robotics taught me many things, and a major part of the learning process were outreaches.

One specific outreach that had an impact was the Cary Scavenger Hunt. I helped with creating a website for the scavenger hunt as well as assisting the judges on the day of the Cary Scavenger Hunt. A big thing I learned was how to meet deadlines and strengthen my teamwork skills. Since there were a lot of people at the Cary Scavenger Hunt, we had to make sure things went smoothly and quickly, and we were able to get through the event with minimal obstructions. Working with the Chief Financial Officer of Cary, we were able to complete the event successfully. I was not only able to help train judges effectively and answer their questions, but I was also able to enjoy the experience with my peers, working together for the smooth execution of Cary Scavenger Hunt. When I helped with the Cary Scavenger Hunt the second year, I knew several people from the previous year. Due to the fact we knew how each of us worked, I experienced more efficiency during the second year. I learned that knowing your teammates can lead to great working relationships and team performance.

The next big event in my life was the transition from middle school to high school. I was anxious about my upcoming adventures, but nonetheless, I was excited. Upon receiving my schedule, and consulting with upperclassmen, I was told I got some of the best teachers. One class, commonly known as C&C (combined Civics and English), was taught by two of the best teachers I have ever had and the best teachers I will ever get. I have grown a lot as a person throughout their class, with a new and unique perspective on life accompanied by a growth of confidence. This class was unique such that both my academic intelligence and emotional intelligence Even though I had an increased workload, I was able to manage my time wisely and perform well in the school; however, I did not have as much free time as I used to.

As I got midway into my freshman year of high school, I had started to slack off. To motivate myself to get my work done as efficiently as possible and stop procrastinating, I reflected upon my leadership learnings about time management and my learning style. After thinking upon it and trying a couple of things, I found out what worked for me.

I devised an acronym for the word "start." The first step is to **S**trategize and plan out what assignments and activities I would do in order. I would also plan out my breaks ahead of time, so I would not get carried away doing something for longer than necessary. Other things I had to plan around were my extracurricular activities and prior engagements. The next step is to **T**ime it out, and to do that I estimate how much time each activity takes me to complete. This gives me an accurate idea of when everything will be finished. The next step is **A**ct to complete, and to do this, I finish my work. I only take a break for the amount of time planned and I eliminate all distractions to maximize the efficiency of my work. After that, I **R**eflect on my actions, to see how well I estimated my time usage. This enables me to recognize my mistakes in time management and use the information to better time my activities for the future. The last thing I do is to **T**ake improved action based on what I have previously learned from the process. This way I am always able to improve my effectiveness.

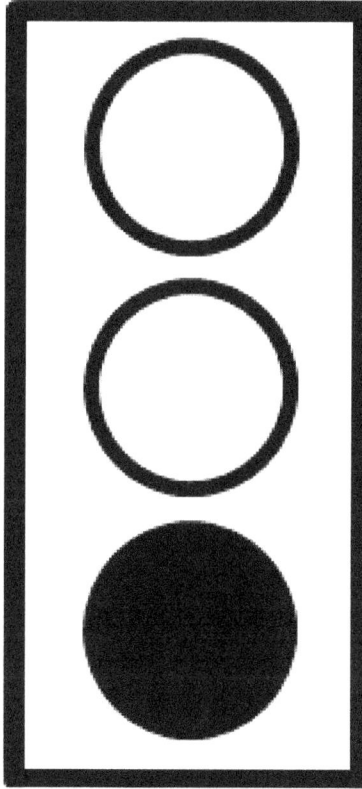

S - Strategize

T - Time it out

A - Act to Complete

R - Reflection on Action

T -Take Improved Action and Repeat

When I was in 9th grade, Coach Divya came across an organization named the Too Much TV (TMT) Youth Foundation. Led by Tamisha Thomas, the youth foundation is creating a curriculum for low-income kids in 1st through 8th grade. The foundation is all about equipping children with leadership, entrepreneurship, website building, photography, and app development based on the STEAM (Science, Technology, Engineering, Art, and Mathematics) principle. The minute I heard about the details of the foundation, I wanted to volunteer and support it because it matched my principles. I went to multiple meetings to learn what the foundation is all about and how it supports the kids. To get supplies such as tablets for children, the foundation uses fundraising. To help, I went to a Cary Scavenger Hunt event with Nehali, who has a chapter later in the book, and we raised money and awareness to support it. Coach Divya and I modified an existing entrepreneurship workshop so that younger kids could get the most out of it. On certain Saturdays, team members and I went to TMT to help teach the entrepreneurial workshop by each leading a group of kids with Coach Divya. We made sure to teach entrepreneurial strategies through fun activities to keep the younger kids engaged. When we asked the students about their takeaways, the insights and wisdom shared by the young kids was impressive and blew me away. When I saw their potential unfold, my enthusiasm doubled my resolve to continue working with them. During the summer, we will continue the entrepreneurial workshop, and help the children develop a business plan through which they will learn to sell products and earn money.

Looking back, I see three major lessons that would have helped me a tremendous amount had I known them when I was younger, so I am going to share them here for younger kids who want to be the best they can and make the world the best it can be. First and foremost, the S.T.A.R.T. concept has helped me tackle my high school workload with time to spare for social and extracurricular activities. Next, knowing that no matter who you are or where you are, you can always be a leader and bring leadership to any situation will help you be more confident when facing challenges. Lastly, learning to understand your teammates when working in a team to achieve a common goal is an important lesson to remember, whether you are doing a project in school or playing a game.

All of my prior experiences have helped me build a solid foundation for a house of leadership. As I continue to lead, I will continue to learn, and overtime my house will become a city. I am enthusiastic about the upcoming journey, and the opportunities awaiting me.

4

Overcoming Leadership
Challenges

*"Lead from the back – and let
others believe they are in front."*

—Nelson Mandela

Middle school is a pretty confusing time, for multiple reasons. You can finally stop being treated like a kid, but you're not really sure that you want to start being treated like an adult just yet. There's just so much baggage that comes along with reaching this age, not to mention all the pressure to fit in. At this age, you're still trying to figure out who you are, and who you want to be. You find yourself overthinking everything and losing control of your emotions for no particular reason. You want to please everyone at once, but you're quickly realizing that it's pretty impossible to do. Basically, the challenge of real life hits you pretty hard in the face when you become a teenager. The good news? You're not the only one.

When I, Nehali, got to middle school, I was pretty scared. I didn't really know anyone in my grade and was convinced I'd end up with no friends. I was afraid to be who I was because I thought that I'd get judged for it. I was shy, soft spoken, and I wasn't the type to stand up for something I wanted. My confidence in myself was severely lacking, and no matter how much I wanted to change that, I knew it wouldn't happen overnight.

Then, one day, my mom told me about an entrepreneurship workshop called Women in Bio that was going to be starting on soon. I'll admit, I was not on board with it at first. It didn't exactly sound like my type of thing, too much having to work with people I didn't know and too far out of my comfort zone. My mom assured me that my sister and a good friend would be going with me and that the workshop would be headed by a close family friend of ours, Coach Divya. This news helped some, but not a lot.

I did end up agreeing to go. I stressed out incessantly until the first workshop, though. What if I had a terrible time? What if I didn't fit in with everyone else? What if I completely embarrassed myself? These thoughts ran through my head constantly.

When I did get there, I saw someone I knew and this made me feel much better; my best friend until the sixth grade just so happened to be attending the workshop too! It definitely allayed fears I had about everyone there being older than me and hating me.

The first thing we did was split into groups. Next, we talked about what exactly entrepreneurship was, and why it was important that we learned about how to handle a startup business. What we would do in the workshop was create our own startup to sell products at a 5k for Cystic Fibrosis. The fact that the money would be raised for Cystic Fibrosis definitely helped everyone in the room get a better perspective about what we were doing. We were suddenly much more inclined to put everything we had into this workshop because we could see ourselves really making a difference.

Within our groups, we began talking about what products we would like to sell. We were given seed money from the coaches to help execute our business plans. I didn't find myself really contributing to the conversation much. I didn't want anyone to judge me based on my ideas. Eventually, we had a list of potential ideas, which we presented to the rest of the groups. Throughout this, the coaches were walking around the room, listening to our ideas and explaining to us how to better build on them.

We decided that we would sell sweatshirts and t-shirts and created a company name, logo, and tagline. While we were making the project, our ideas didn't quite work out and we had to find a new product to make. We settled on polo shirts and water bottles as our final products.

Team Building

One thing I noticed is that our team worked together very well, as it didn't take us very long to realize that compromise was the only way we would get things done. Another reason we worked so well together had to do with the way we decided the leadership of the group. Coach Divya had given us the idea of switching up who would be the leader of the group on a given day. When things weren't working out within our group, I looked through my notes and suggested that we try her method. This way, everyone got their ideas heard and creating cohesive plans was much easier. I noticed of the other groups that they didn't work as well together, as there was much more fighting over ideas, but that too lessened up after a couple more workshops.

The next step was financing everything in order to see how our ideas would work logistically. What we learned was how precisely everything needed to be calculated and even though it wasn't a big deal in a workshop setting, a small miscalculation could be a serious problem for an actual company. This led to some disagreements over what was more important and what our priorities were, but once again, due to the way that our group worked together and the way we split up leadership, the problems were solved with little trouble and everyone ended up satisfied.

Very soon, I found myself looking forward to the workshops every week, something I never thought would happen. I dedicated time outside of the workshop towards planning and improving my skills, which still prove invaluable today. The fact that everyone within our group took the time to look at our ideas outside of the workshop and work out the smaller problems gave us the opportunity to iron out the bigger issues within the workshop and allowed for us to be much more productive.

Having Strong Leaders Breeds Strong Leadership

During the whole process, the coaches were invaluable. They gave advice on how to improve upon our own ideas, but they didn't give us the answers to our problems. They instead gave us the tools to be able to work it out ourselves, helping us to really take away lasting lessons from the workshop.

One workshop, we had guest speakers come in and talk about their own startup business, a local fruit company. They explained the struggle to get their business off the ground, but how they overcame their challenges and came out better for it. Even though they still did face daily struggles with their business, they never let it stop them from moving ahead. Currently, they own a successful business in the Triangle that continues to grow each day.

Implementing What Was Learned

Before we knew it, it was D-Day, the day of the 5K. We came to the 5K at about 6 AM to set up, and while everyone was pretty tired, it was canceled out by the nervousness and excitement. We set up our products on tables outside, and despite the freezing weather, we had a good time together. Somehow, over the course of those workshops, we had become good friends within our groups. Then, the race began.

At first of course, we didn't have any real sales, and though we understood that it was due to the cold, it was still a little bit disheartening.

After the 5K ended, a little girl with Cystic Fibrosis came before everyone who participated in the run. She knew she would only live until age thirty or thirty-five, and she couldn't have been more than seven. She talked about how she felt about the walk and how grateful she was that everyone was coming together to raise money to find a cure for people like her. She told us how things like this walk gave her hope that one day there would be a cure, if not for her, then for people in the future. Almost four years later, I still remember every single word of her speech.

After hearing her speech, we looked at our sales a different way. We saw how much of a difference our actions could make to help contribute towards the discovery of a cure for that girl and others like her. Her bravery in the face of her disease was truly inspiring to everyone who heard it. She refused to give up hope or to give in to her disease, instead doing what made her truly happy and living life as a normal child.

We continued sales well after the race ended. More people than I ever imagined were interested in our products and what we were doing. The fact that we had made the business from scratch helped us sell the product with more enthusiasm and with more pride in our work. After the last people finally dwindled away, we counted up our profits and were shocked to find that we had made over two hundred dollars. Every single penny of it was donated towards research for a Cystic Fibrosis cure.

The Importance of Leadership

The workshop was a milestone in my life for helping boost my self-confidence and was an amazing opportunity to give back to the community. I could finally see that I could make a difference. The benefits that came from working with my team are still with me.

As my leadership journey continued, my mom told me about another workshop with Coach Divya, a leadership course, about a year after the entrepreneurship workshop. I was wary at first, but once again I had the assurance of there being people I knew in attendance. In the first class, I realized that there were just a small group of people, almost none of whom I actually knew well, besides my sister and another friend. I was intimidated at first, but the other girls were friendly and we started talking easily.

One of the first things we did in the workshop was learn about something that just about every teenager out there suffers from: procrastination. Honestly, at that time, I was the worst at procrastination. I didn't start anything until the very last minute, causing me to stay up until 2 or 3 AM every night for pretty much no reason, which led to problems with other aspects of my life.

One of the activities we did that really stuck with me was a priorities chart, which divided up things into four categories: urgent, important, urgent and important, and neither. We made a list of things that we felt took priority, but after being urged by Coach Divya to take another look at it, we saw that the things we thought had to get done first, were really just things that we needed to keep in our minds in order to complete them. For example, an urgent and important activity would be that science project due tomorrow that you haven't started (which has definitely happened to everyone). However, while you probably really do need to clean your room, it's not as urgent, and should be saved for when you have time.

Throughout the workshop, there were older students with us who had already been through the leadership program. They worked closely with us to help develop our skills, and they told personal stories, which helped us grow as well.

We continued through the classes working on many useful skills like time management, organization (another weakness of mine), and leadership skills. I found myself growing more responsible and paying more attention to prioritizing my work, which saved me a ton of time. Coach Divya pushed us to grow not only as individual leaders, but together as teammates also.

She created a buddy system, in which we would set specific goals and then join up with a partner in order to help each other stay on track with them. There would be three goals. One was a personal goal; mine was to keep my room clean. The next was to offer strangers the small gift of a smile. This collective goal was to smile at five new people a day, since you never know how it helps brighten someone's bad day. Finally, we set a goal to help the people in our community. We started off small, and I resolved to start mentoring students in band.

Now, for a bunch of 8-9th graders to keep these goals and remember to uphold them was a challenging thing. So, Coach Divya came up with an idea that would not only keep us on track, but also help us with our partnership skills. Every time one of us found the other slipping behind, or not quite following through on our goals, we would constantly nag the other until we could pick up the pace on our work. This activity really helped us grow closer as a group, as we were able to work better with each other and understood each other better. Three years later, my buddy and I still remain friends.

Discovering the Leader Inside of You

One particular moment in the workshop that I remember most clearly was when I finally came out of my shell. In school, we had been working on a Constitution project. The whole school would take different parts of the Constitution and make a video rendition of it. I'll add here that I hated all of these projects, as they all involved putting myself out there and being a little weird, but that was just how our school was. The whole project was pretty ridiculous, and it was meant to be a light and funny project that we could look back on and laugh at, and surprisingly learn something along the way. It involved some pretty out of the box thinking and you had to be pretty spontaneous. Unfortunately, spontaneous was not something I liked at all. A portion of this project was a song and dance choreographed to a rendition of the preface to the Constitution. I hated it since I always felt offbeat and awkward when we rehearsed in class.

In the leadership workshop we were talking one day, and I happened to mention this project. Coach Divya then asked if I could show the dance to the rest of the people there. I'll admit, I really didn't want to, but I eventually did. The dance was pretty out there and included some hilarious moves and we ended up laughing the whole time. I somehow ended up teaching the rest of them how to do it, which was not what I expected. We were all laughing at each other's attempts to do it and it escalated into everyone coming up with some random crazy dance routine and then teaching it to everyone.

Finally, the workshop came to an end, but there was still one more thing to do. We had to give a presentation to our families about the workshop itself. Everyone would give an individual presentation. We spent about a week working on these presentations, and I could tell that everyone, including myself, was nervous for these. We rehearsed them in front of each other, in front of Coach Divya, and in front of the student mentors as well. When the time came, we found we were so well prepared and that we had overcome many of our presentation insecurities during the workshop itself, that one presentation didn't seem like such a big deal.

After the workshop concluded, I found myself to be much stronger, in terms of leadership ability. I was no longer as afraid to give class presentations, and I look forward to them now. I didn't have as much of a problem with group projects and taking control, and I became much more outgoing going into high school the next year.

Last year, I was given the opportunity to work more with the 1/1/1 Leadership Project, which I had started in the Leadership Workshop the previous year. At a local scavenger hunt in the fall, Rishi and I created a presentation and talked to people about the 1/1/1 Project. It worked out a lot better than either of us thought, and we pledged multiple people to commit to the project, and donate money, which then went to a charity.

Continued Growth

Now, as I head into the 11th grade, I find myself with another opportunity to help my community and to grow as a leader. The Too-Much TV (TMT) Youth Foundation helps kids from underserved backgrounds grow as leaders and students. Over the summer, I look forward to the opportunity to work with these students and help them grow. In October, there will be a community walk, where there will be a fundraiser for this program. I've pledged to get twenty people to sign up for the walk by then.

When I wrote this chapter, it was a lot harder than I originally thought. I had to rewrite it several times before finding something that worked. However, as I wrote, I grew closer with the other writers, some of whom I'd never met before. Over the past few months, we've gone from strangers, to a team, to friends. As I wrote this chapter, I kept in mind what I would say to my own Middle School self, what kinds of advice I would have for the person I was then, and other people who may feel the same way I did. Here are some of the things I came up with:

Middle School is everyone's awkward phase, it's not just you. Don't worry about what other people think about you, or about embarrassing yourself, because they're probably worrying the same thing.

You don't have to change the world, or cure cancer, to make a difference. You can do that just by doing small acts of kindness for other people. Smile at someone on the street, or help them when they're down. It may not make a difference to you, but you never know how it might help them.

Use your time better. You don't want to wake up one day and realize that you've wasted some of the best years of your life. Challenge yourself and set goals outside your comfort zone that push you to become a better person.

If you set goals for yourself, follow through with them. It doesn't matter what it is. Keep your room clean, or finish that project a little bit early. Time management is going to be everything in the next few years, and you'll learn that the hard way if you don't start now.

It'll all work out. Everything seems crazy now and the future seems impossible, but you're going to be fine.

5

To the Stars

"The only person you are destined to become
is the person you decide to be."

—Ralph Waldo Emerson

It was a normal practice for the varsity volleyball team: arrive at 3:30, three laps around the gym to warm up, start stretching at 3:40, and in full practice swing by 4:00.

Surprisingly, the entire team was present. With three concussions, two ankle sprains and one knee injury, the team had been through enough to destroy any other team, yet we still worked harder. Determined to have a team stronger than any other, a season greater than any before, and to be the best player I, Catherine, could be I pushed harder and harder, diving for each ball and sprinting for each hit…until I stumbled on the court, a sharp pain shooting through my ankle.

Now, ankle injuries are nothing new to me. Having two sprains already under my belt, I knew what a real injury felt like, and this was nothing more than a twist of the ankle—right? I shook off the pain and jumped back on the court, but the injury persisted. Frustrated and upset, I realized that there was nothing left to do but get my ankle checked out. If I didn't know what was wrong with my ankle, I might inadvertently make the injury worse.

I visited to the doctor a few days later, and was referred to physical therapy…for the third time in a year and a half. I wouldn't be able to play for the rest of the season; I'd have to be relegated to a manager position. I wouldn't be able to reach my goal of becoming varsity libero. Obviously, I was disappointed, angry, and frustrated. Little did I know that such a setback would turn into one of the most exciting opportunities I've ever encountered.

I arrived at my physical therapy office on a cool September afternoon, resentful and dreading my session. I'd just gotten out of physical therapy from my last ankle sprain six months ago; was it really necessary for me to come back and miss the rest of the season? Apparently, it was.

My appointment was scheduled for 3:40. I was ten minutes early, so I sat down to wait for my therapist. Many of the other patients had their heads buried in magazines or books, iPads or phones, so I took a seat in the farthest corner possible.

As soon as I sat down, the office door swung open again, and in walked a smiling teenage girl. I was surprised to see such an excited face—patients aren't normally excited to go to physical therapy! She signed in at the front desk, looked around at the surrounding patients, looked straight at me, smiled again, strode over and took the seat directly across from me.

Upon meeting her, the first thing I noticed was a lanyard around her neck, bearing an ID with the title "Intern." I asked her about her internship, and her eyes lit up. She was so excited to be interning for the PT office, she said, and she couldn't wait to see what the day held in store.

I could truly see that she was passionate about what she was doing, and it struck a nerve with me. For months I'd been thinking about internships, something that I could do to demonstrate my skills, to find my passion and grow as an individual. We talked for a few more minutes about internships, and how we truly believed in their power as an introduction into the working world, as well as an exercise in finding our fortes. I spoke about my dreams of becoming an engineer, of eventually connecting my math and science skills to business, of being able to influence others in the most effective ways possible.

She was then called to meet her mentor, one of the physical therapists, and we had to say goodbye. I watched her stride with nearly tangible confidence over to her employer, shake hands with him, and smile brightly. She was on her way…but I was still stuck.

I didn't know where to go for such experience. How could I possibly act on my dreams now? How was I supposed to find an internship that would help me get experience in my desired fields? How would I find a program that spoke to my soul, enabling me to grow as a leader?

That's when I met Coach Divya.

Also a patient at the PT office, Coach Divya had overheard part of our conversation. She'd listened to me speak passionately about my desires for an internship; my motivation to help others; my understanding of how you (or anyone!) can truly make a difference in other peoples' lives, no matter how young or "inexperienced" you may be. She was wondering if I'd be interesting in applying for an internship position with her company, the DP Group.

We talked for a few minutes, until I was called to my appointment, and she then gave me her contact information. I looked forward to calling her, so we could further discuss my aspirations and goals within an internship.

I was ecstatic—I could barely focus on what my physical therapist was saying. Who would've thought that such an incredible opportunity would come from such an ordinary, mundane conversation? At the same time, though, I was incredibly nervous. Apart from babysitting and the occasional community project, I'd never been a part of such an influential work experience, and I didn't really know what to expect. As a high schooler, I'd never considered that I could actually make a difference; I could step out of my "schoolwork bubble" and make waves in different ways. So, I entered my internship with Coach Divya a little apprehensive, but still anticipating the best.

The Constellation Principle

Before I recount my journey, I want to share with you the most important concept I've learned throughout my entire internship: The Constellation Principle, an idea designed by Coach Divya.

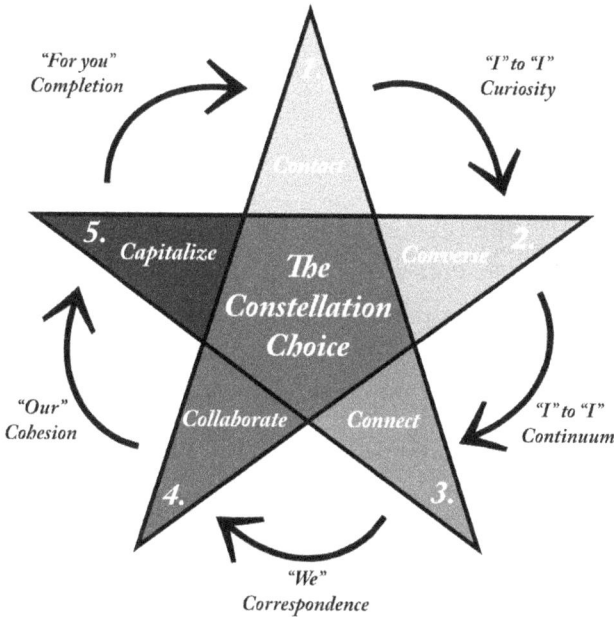

"For you"
Completion

"I" to "I"
Curiosity

5.
Capitalize

Converse **2.**

The
Constellation
Choice

Contact

"Our"
Cohesion

Collaborate   *Connect*

"I" to "I"
Continuum

4.

3.

"We"
Correspondence

This is the illustration of the growth and development you experience within every relationship, from your first meeting (contact) to the final product of your collaboration (capitalize). Everything I've been able to do in my internship has occurred according to this concept, and it's been incredibly fulfilling to be able to see each facet of this relationship develop.

In every relationship you have, from classmates to teachers and eventually to employers, your goal is to transgress through these five steps and create something amazing out of your relationship—be it a project, a presentation, or even a book. Following the Constellation Principle was amazingly fulfilling and empowering for me, and noticing the development of your relationship transformed me from an apprehensive and nervous individual to a confident and enabled student and employee. This transformation can happen to anyone!

Granted, it's not an overnight change. It's more of a gradual shift, occurring over days, weeks, and even months of your experiences through school, friendships and family. I'll share with you my journey and describe what I've learned, both inside my internship journey and in other contexts as well. Then, the rest is up to you—take control!

Step One: Contact

I remember vividly the first time I met with Coach Divya. It was the fall of my junior year, my volleyball fiasco had finally terminated, and my ankle was slowly but surely healing. The sky was overcast and there was a slight breeze, but it wasn't too cold—perfect outside weather. When I arrived at her office, Coach Divya had the idea to have our first meeting outside so we could enjoy the wonderful weather while discussing our ideas.

There was a walking trail she particularly enjoyed, so we thought it'd be a good idea to walk that path and get to know each other before the internship truly began. We talked about her expectations for my work and the kind of material I would be producing, and I began to see the full extent of the positive impact I could make. This was the first time I realized the connection I had made with Coach Divya, and that truly great things could come from our relationship. The curiosity sparked by our conversation at the physical therapy office had led to a greater opportunity to come together and create a great friendship, a fantastic base that all our subsequent accomplishments would grow from.

The connection is the most important part of building beneficial relationships. Without the initial encounter at physical therapy and the following introductory meeting that fall morning, the rest of the relationship wouldn't have been able to take place, rendering my experience of the Constellation Principle nonexistent.

When I realized that the first step of the Constellation Principle was taking place inside my internship, I began to look for contact in my other endeavors, because you experience this process in any relationship. In my case, the next aspect of my life that I could clearly see this principle outlined was in my yearbook class. As design editor, it was up to me and my fellow editors to make incredibly important decisions about the yearbook. This time, the question about what colors the yearbook would have was brought into play. My co-editors and I called a meeting to contact the other editors, and to establish a jumping-off point for the rest of our ideas. Without this meeting being held, the yearbook would have reached a dilemma, as the Constellation Principle couldn't have taken place and a decision couldn't have been reached.

In my experience, there are a few tips that can help you achieve your goals if you're looking for reaching for reaching this first connection:

Be open to any opportunities! Just keep an eye out for potential beneficial relationships, whether it be a friendship or work relationship. Bear in mind that meeting anybody could be the start of your next incredible endeavor.

Make sure you're demonstrating your best self. I know there's a big emphasis placed on apathy and negativity right now, but if you're looking to grow as an individual and be a part of an inspirational project, you have to always make sure you're on your best behavior. You never know who could be an employer looking for a new applicant, a teacher looking for an assistant, or a classmate looking for a partner for a project. Every new encounter is a chance to make a great first impression!

Always be sure to follow up. You can be the most skilled musician, rhythmic dancer or versed performer, but if you can't close loops with your acquaintances and respond promptly to their requests, you won't remain their coworkers for very long. By responding promptly and taking the first step in establishing a good relationship, you can prove your responsibility and orga-nization to any potential clients or colleagues. If Coach Divya and I hadn't had our meeting following our initial encounter at the physical therapy office, the connection would have dissi-pated and this book wouldn't exist!

These are the three most important principles to follow within the "contact" step. If you keep these three key concepts in mind, more opportunities than you could ever dream of will present themselves to you! And remember: confidence and a smile can take you miles.

Step 2: Converse

When Coach Divya and I returned from our walking meeting, we were both excited for what collaborative opportunities lay ahead. She had some projects she needed help with and wanted to include me on, such as learning different webinar programs and recording her "Writing Your Message" series. The first challenge was confronting the multiple webinar platforms. Prior to meeting Coach Divya, my work had been fully laid out for me: projects were fully explained, deadlines were laid out weeks in advance, and if I had any questions I could go straight to my teachers and get answers. However, I had no resources to access this time around—I was fully responsible for learning the software on my own, and then mak-ing tutorial videos for Coach Divya to learn from.

The independence aspect of this project was incredibly important, sure. Having the confidence to trust yourself and explore new possibili-ties in your learning is always key, but your knowledge is worthless if you can't talk about what you've discovered.

After weeks of studying the programs, learning how to upload pre-made videos, record live webinars and interact with clients through the software, it came time to relay what I'd learned to Coach Divya. This was the "converse" part of our relationship; before we could start working towards our goals, we had to discuss what we knew about required pro-grams and information.

Being able to recount what I'd learned and explaining my process to Coach Divya really opened my eyes to the importance of conversation in a relationship. To be able to fully reach your collaborative potential, ensuring that you and your colleague are on the same page is incredibly important! Setting the stage for efficient partnership is absolutely essential in formulating a great relationship, and helps you develop a status as a mature, cooperative individual.

Opening my heart to this new stage of our relationship helped me look forward to the next step in my yearbook endeavor. After our initial contact, the editorial group established a series of meetings to articulate our color ideas in order to get everybody on the same page. In this stage, everyone had equal voices. We didn't have to select any specific color schemes yet, we were just brainstorming. This step was incredibly important in leveling the playing field, opening up opportunities to shape the nature of the book. Without this step, a lot of creative potential would have been lost.

Finally, I'd love to condense all of my learning on this relationship step down into a few absolutely essential points.

Have faith in yourself when you're learning something new.
Before you can begin to converse about your strong points and discuss their applications, you need to be sure you've fully mastered your material. It can be frustrating at times, especially when you're working with new software and you're not receiving direct help from anyone, but you have to remain patient with yourself and remember that you're learning a new skill and you need to be able to discuss the joint applications of your new abilities!

Be sure to be complete in your explanations, addressing all benefits and the potential downfalls. It's incredibly important to outline the importance of the new skill(s), especially when it can accelerate the completion of your project or make the process much simpler. For me, learning multiple webinar softwares allowed me to discern which program worked best for our needs. Revealing my findings showed that I had fully encapsulated every potential application of the software and addressed every possible concern that might arise as we worked on the project. This attention to detail and thoroughness strengthened our bond of trust and demonstrated my responsibility.

Create any necessary supplementary material to address any potential subsequent questions or concerns. While face-to-face conversation is ideal, sometimes it's not possible to personally interface with your colleagues. In my case, I got the chance to make tutorial videos about the webinar software. You could also utilize step-by-step explanations, a reference regarding the software, or anything else you want—just make sure that it's helpful to your coworkers and might answer any further questions they have. By being complete about relaying information and discussing future work, you demonstrate your accountability and thoroughness.

Step Three: Connect

After I'd finished relaying everything I learned and Coach Divya had finished watching my tutorial videos, we were finally ready to begin our work together. Coach Divya had been working on a project for a while called the "Writing Your Message" program. Learning the webinar software and collaborating to work with more video software was the final piece needed to finish this project. Before we could start though, we had to lay out the project framework and make sure we had all of the necessary knowledge and resources to fully reach the project's potential.

We sat down one afternoon and made an outline of the project, designating a timeline for certain aspects of the program to be completed. After that, it was far clearer what we needed to still do to accomplish the rest of the series; this connection was just what I needed to set the project efforts into full throttle.

Picture the connection in this way: your teacher assigns you a long-term group project, assigns your workmates, and gives you full control over your project type and timeline. After you've made contact with the rest of your group and conversed about what steps you need to take to prepare for your assignment, you can truly then begin to connect under your common goal before beginning work. During this connection, you make your plan for finishing the project on time; day by day, you discern what you need to do to keep your project on track. It's only when you've bonded and created a comfortable and productive environment that you can enter your next stage of your relationship.

Applying this notion to the yearbook environment, the rest of the editors and I had a conversation about what we specifically wanted for our book. Putting all ideas aside, we came up with "ideal books," books that had the perfect vibe, beautiful colors, and descriptive fonts. Having this conversation about what people jointly and individually desired was eye-opening, and from that point we could designate tasks to the proper editors. We then set plans for developing the rest of the book, designating deadlines, and making sure we were all on the same page before we brainstormed our final product.

Before we move on, let's condense this entire process down into a couple of easy-to-remember points:

Be complete in your planning. Be sure not to leave any important aspects out of your discussion! One missed point and you might create a big problem, and the biggest part of this connection point is to establish the plan for your project.

Make sure you've got all the needed resources from the previous step. Before moving on to the connection step, you've got to be absolutely sure that you were complete in the conversation aspect of the relationship. If you missed anything, you've got to go back and fill any missing holes to make sure your plan can be reasonably fulfilled.

Keep it real! Don't set goals that are completely out of your reach—be sure that you've chosen a reasonable plan, one that's not overwhelming or unattainable. The next step of your relationship, the collaboration aspect, will be much more difficult for you and your colleagues if you set impossible goals for your group. You'll end up making everybody nervous, angry and frustrated, and even potentially damage your relationship!

The next step is what all of the previous steps have been leading up to: collaboration!

Step 4: Collaboration

Congratulations! With the contact made, your conversations held and the connection established, you're finally ready to collaborate with your coworkers and start working toward your final goal! This is one of the most fulfilling aspects of the Constellation Principle (besides revealing your final product) because you finally get to see the physical result of all the work you've put into your relationship. Not only that, but being able to work together constructively with your colleagues helps further build your confidence and belief in yourself, as it did for me.

It was in this step when Coach Divya and I put down our planners and picked up our computers. Coach Divya had been teaching me for several months on how to become more confident and grow meaningful relationships through The Constellation Principle. Additionally, she coached me on writing my chapter for this book using her "Write Your Message" book writing program, a series that she actually had me help develop by writing the scripts. Writing the scripts about my experience for the video narration was time consuming and different than any other previous project I'd experienced, and it was at times difficult for both of us to meet. Obviously, school didn't stop for me, and she had responsibilities other than this project.

That being said, realizing the dedication needed to finish creating the "Write Your Message" project gave me another level of accountability and confidence. Sure, I still had my old responsibilities of schoolwork, babysitting, everything that most teenagers face, but now I had a much bigger project that I still needed to attend to. For a while, balancing all the aspects of my life was a difficult task, but realizing the importance of finishing this project fully, striving for the final step, and exploring co-creation, was what drove me to push all obstacles aside, sit down and crank the project out with Coach Divya.

At first, the concept of helping with a program like the "Writing Your Message" series was very intimidating to me- I truly had never done anything as substantial as working with products that were going to be used by people outside my immediate circle of friends and colleagues! Fear and apprehension were definitely still there at the beginning, and truthfully still remained present throughout some of the previous relationship levels—and that's okay! When confronting a giant task that you've never experienced before, you're going to be nervous, and sometimes you'll feel like your goal is unattainable. Trust me though, just setting your sights on your final project can do wonders for your motivation and confidence. I realized at this point when I had "just started" to begin working on the project that I'd truly been putting in a lot of hard work from the beginning. Make no mistake, even making that initial contact can be pretty tough! Realizing how far I'd come from the beginning of our relationship and pushing through any remaining apprehension was what fueled me at this point in our relationship, and drove me to work hard with Coach Divya to finish out the project.

After I realized what great progress Coach Divya and I had made in this stage of our relationship, I took my new skillset once more to the yearbook classroom. With the confidence that the other editors and I would be able to address our differences and collaborate to find a design that we all loved, I entered our editors meeting feeling energized and excited for our book. We were able to work through any disagreements that arose in earlier stages, and I was even able to bring up a basic color scheme that everybody enjoyed! Collaborating on these aspects of our book and determining what everybody wanted was imperative in not only developing our book, but also solidifying our friendships and empowering us to make bigger decisions in the future.

Since this stage is one of the biggest aspects of the Constellation Principle, and one of the more labor-intensive steps you'll encounter, let's recap:

- **Realize how far you've come.** As I said before, you've come so far already! It's important to recognize what you've done in your relationship so far—good for you! Now that you've done all the requisite work you can work on making your dreams come true.

- **Just don't let it go to your head.** Although you've made some amazing progress already by this point in the Constellation Principle, you can't be complacent with the work you've already done. Always strive to fully realize your dreams, don't settle for less than you've dreamed of. You can always find ways to make your work even better.

- **Don't let fear paralyze you—dive in!** When you're working on the project itself, sometimes very difficult aspects of the project will present themselves. You may be tempted to give up at times. I know I was tempted to abandon a webinar software or stop tweaking a frustrating picture. Sometimes you'll hit a roadblock and you don't feel like you can do anything, but you can't be stuck in one place forever. Acknowledge your apprehension, address the problem, and go from there! That way, be it a difficult math assignment or a relationship issue, you'll be able to move forward from your dilemma and keep building your future.

And now, on to our final step…

Step Five: Capitalize

You're done!

This is the absolute final step of the Constellation Principle, in which you and your fellow coworkers can see the product of all of your work. Well done!

This step is one of the most fulfilling. Without any further planning or work to be done, you can just step back and admire what you've created through your relationship. It's like finishing a final school project that you've been working on for months, an essay that you've finessed and dissected for ages before finally turning it in. Not only have you reached an end to your project, but you've experienced new processes; made new connections; and grown as a student, friend, and coworker.

Usually, when you see the term "capitalize" in use, it's in regards to financial gain. While you may make money off of your final product, depending on the nature of your project, when I say "capitalize", I mean in terms of making the most of your relationship. At this final stage in your partnership, you and your coworkers have made the absolute most of your time and effort—you've truly capitalized your relationship!

I've shared with you how I've seen the Constellation Principle in action in one of the greatest experiences I've had. Perhaps this is one of the most step-by-step examples of the principle, and it's the aspect of my life where I could most clearly observe the transition from contact to converse, from connect to collaborate, and finally, to capitalize.

Like the final yearbook that would ultimately be produced by the yearbook staff, this book is the product of the Constellation Principle: the capitalization of all our hard work and dedication. I've worked with Coach Divya, Rishi, Nehali, Tatianna and Varun to share our efforts with you, and bring you the best of our accomplishments.

I love that I've had the opportunity to meet Coach Divya and be mentored by her in order to inspire others to reach their full potential as I realize my own. It's been incredible to see myself grow as a leader, in terms of confidence and responsibility. It's difficult for many teens to grasp the concepts needed to secure positive relationships and work effectively with other people because we don't get firsthand work experience outside of school. I know that the traits I've developed will help me in connecting with professors at college, discussing project with peers, and even during job interviews!

If I had to reduce everything I've learned to three takeaway points, it'd have to be something along these lines:

Leaders really aren't born, they're made! It's true; at the beginning of this project I was still apprehensive, more willing to follow than lead. However, through experiencing the Constellation Principle, I've seen myself grow tremendously in terms of confidence, efficiency and responsibility. Leading an ear, a helping hand, or even just a simple smile can change how not only others perceive you, but how you view yourself as well. It really doesn't take much to establish that initial contact and to open up a relationship that could take you anywhere.

Be sure you're making the most out of your relationship. This sounds weird at first glance, but I'm just saying to make sure that you're doing everything you can to strengthen your relationship, because the deeper the connection, the better the capitalization will ultimately be. By making sure that you're always on the same page and doing everything you can to ensure your final product is great, and that you're setting yourself up for tremendous success.

It's not all be fun and games. I know I've described this process as smooth sailing, and for me, it has mostly been. I'm very fortunate to have wonderful peers who respect my opinions while still cherishing their own, but this won't always be the case. You might meet people who, despite everything you try, hold their views in higher regard than yours. It can be difficult to even contact these individuals. You might be uncomfortable at first, but with enough effort you can reach them; it might just take some time at first.

Thank you so much for reading! Now, you're all set to take advantage of any opportunities that come your way. Go out there and make a difference!

5

Kindness Chapter

"Be kind whenever possible. It is always possible."

—Dalai Lama

While writing this book, we had many great experiences together as a team. All of us went from complete strangers to a team in a matter of months. Some of these experiences translated into something more, resulting in this chapter.

One day in February 2016, we were working on our chapters together, and figuring out some details for our individual work. We were discussing the 1/1/1 Leader Project, and its relation to our work. One thing we talked about a lot were the small acts of kindness that were such a central part of the project. The entire premise of the 1/1/1 Leader Project is small, random acts of kindness that help better our communities, and help bring people closer together. In a world that seems to be lacking in empathy, kindness integrates communities in a way that not much else can.

As Coach Divya soon informed us, February happened to be the month of kindness. After talking about this for a while, the team and Coach Divya came up with an idea. We decided that we would look at other people's random acts of kindness, and see how it affected them, and would dedicate a chapter of the book to telling these stories.

Each team member reached out to their friends, and we asked them about any random act of kindness that they remember performing, and how it affected them personally. While not all people took the question seriously, and some had no answer for us, many did, and we were left with stories of selflessness and kindness in many forms. Below we have compiled the stories that we got from our peers over the course of the month. Names have been omitted to retain confidentiality of the writers.

One memorable act of kindness that I remember was in India when I visited a homeless shelter and helped volunteer there for some time, by aiding the people and donating items. It has affected me because I started to understand that I should be thankful for what I have that many others may not have.

I helped with an autistic camp. It opened my eyes to what the teachers sacrifice to help these kids have fun.

I helped at miracle league which is a baseball league that is for mentally ill or disabled children. It has made me feel good about myself and more inclined to help others.

After signing for 1/1/1 Leader Project, I was thinking about kindness. One day, we were returning from Chick-Fil- A with lot of food. As we stopped at the stoplight, I saw a homeless man sitting on the curb. I looked at my mom and asked her if I could give my food to the homeless guy. She nodded her head and I gave the gentleman a Chic-Fil-A sandwich with drink and fries. His big smile said it all.

So I don't entirely know if this is a "random act" of kindness, but when I was in 2nd grade, I sold muffins and lemonade at my mom's company to earn money to buy Christmas presents for a family in need that my class was sponsoring at the time. I remember that (with a contribution that morning from my dad) I earned exactly $100 total and went to the drug store to pick out cool toys for the several children in the family. I think that I was definitely proud of myself and excited to help, but I remember my 2nd grade teacher finding out that I had raised all of the money myself and how proud she was of me and that just made me so happy. She was such a role model in my life and she was proud of me for buying kids presents!

I haven't really made the connection until just now, but that may be part of why I go to Target every year to buy Christmas presents for a kid in need. It's so fun, and I use a good bit of my own money and I love to try and just spoil whatever kid we are shopping for because I know that the kids in the foster care system that we're shopping for most likely don't have many opportunities where someone spoils them and buys them not only what they need, but also fun things like toys and books.

Recently, I have been talking to the school dining staff. After conversing with one of the women about how her week was going, she told me that she had a lot of stressful schoolwork to complete, but she was looking forward to her birthday that Friday. The next day I made a handwritten card wishing her a happy birthday, and presented it to her on her birthday at lunch. Seeing the smile on her face made me feel like I had made an impact, and it made my day to have made hers.

One time I had a meaningful conversation with one of my friends. She was going through a hard time and needed someone to talk to. I like that I was able to be her safe place and someone she could be vulnerable with—without the fear of judgment. This experience really helped put the minor things that I complain about in perspective. It helped me realize that people really can be going through more than I might think. Overall, I've just made it a point to be more kind to the people around me.

After my friend went through a tough breakup with her boyfriend of three years, I brought her a TARDIS cookie jar (from Doctor Who, her favorite show), full of Jolly Ranchers, her favorite candy, to try and cheer her up! She still has it in her room, and it really helped her get through that tough time.

APUSH is a very difficult class for a lot of the students in my school, but it's always been relatively easy for me- I've got an affinity for history and I really enjoy it. For the first big test, a lot of students were really struggling with the material. Since I was okay with the class so far, I made a study guide and provided everybody with good studying materials, and made sure to be there to answer their questions. I've done that for every test since, and everybody really appreciates the help! It's nice being able to help others with understanding difficult material.

Physics has always been a relatively easy subject for me; moreover, I really enjoy exploring different topics. However, I've got a friend in my class who's been having a rough time with the material, so I asked her if we could meet after school so I could outline the basics for her. We did a couple problems together and then I watched her do a couple herself to make sure she understood the material, and now she's able to work these difficult problems herself!

One particular memorable act of kindness that I have done is when I stayed with one of my friends at a dance until her parent arrived. Personally, I don't like leaving any one of my team members behind when I can leave at any time that I want to. Seeing what happens to some teenage girls in this world when it becomes dark, I don't feel comfortable leaving kids that are 14-16 years old alone. This has affected my outlook on optimism and altruism by showing me that there are some ways to help others that don't cost a cent. Not only did she appreciate it as she drove away, but her father did as well as they drove away waving to me. Looking after others whether they are friends, family, or teammates is simple, yet extremely important. Overall, this act of kindness opened my eyes to the simple tasks one can do for the safety and security of fellow members in society that don't cost anything but time.

One particular act of kindness I remember was when my friend Julia was incredibly stressed over her physics final, so I took time out of my free period to make her hot chocolate and practice her formulas with her. It really seemed to help calm her down before her test, and I was happy to have made a difference in her feeling prepared for the test, even if it was just a little presence! She came up and hugged me after her test, thanking me for taking a little bit of time out to help her, because it made a huge difference in her confidence and happiness.

One particular act of kindness that I remember was standing up for a kid in seventh grade when she was getting bullied. I remember walking outside and seeing a lot of people making fun of her. I went and told her that none of the stuff they were saying was true and I helped her talk to a teacher about the incident. This really showed me how standing up for someone can help them not feel like a victim and it showed me that we can all make a change.

I paid for a random person at Starbucks when they didn't have enough money to get their coffee

---

I donated money and food to the Home for Boys and Girls. I felt like I helped someone live a good and healthy life.

When I went to India, near a temple, there were many beggars that stand outside the temple. There were around 20 of them, and most of them are completely destitute. The next day, when I went to the temple, I gave each man 100 rupees and a T-shirt, and each woman a 100 rupees and a sari. All of them were so happy afterwards, and it felt really good to give them something. This affected my way of looking at optimism, by realizing that you get so much happiness and just a lot of energy from helping others. It showed me that you can get so much happiness by caring for others rather than yourself all the time.

My first friend is the sweetest girl you will ever meet. She has always been sweet, loving, and caring to everyone. So, for the month of February she decided to take her kindness up a notch. She took time out of her busy schedule, bought small pieces of candy, and taped the pieces of candy to almost everyone's locker at our school. I was talking to her after the month was over to see how she thought she did, and I will never forget, she just looked at me and smiled. That smile symbolized that it doesn't make much time to make someone's day.

Spreading kindness doesn't mean you have to buy things to impress others. It can be by just smiling at someone or even saying 'hi' to someone you don't normally talk to. This girl in my class is very shy; I have only heard her talk maybe once or twice, but when I talked to her about the month dedicated to kindness, she was all for it. Sometimes, all you need is just a push. I was very proud of her, she made this month into a challenge. Every time I saw her in the hallway, she would smile at someone or give them a compliment. Now, that may not seem like a huge deal, but for her it was because she went out of her comfort zone not only for herself, but for others too.

People have different ways of spreading kindness. It can be through a note, a smile, or even by a simple hello. One of my friends took kindness to a whole new level. Not only did she give smiles and compliments, every morning she would tweet an inspirational quote. Her idea was to give a quote that would make everyone's day great! This was a great idea because when we wake up what do we all do? Go on social media. She wanted to be the reason people had smiles on their faces. By doing this simple action, she motivated not only myself, but others too.

At the beginning of March, I asked her how February went for her and she said it couldn't have gone any better. I know by doing this, it put a smile not only on her face, but on other people's faces around the world.

Now every week she will put an inspirational or a motivational quote on her Twitter and close to a hundred people re-tweet it. See how simple it is share kindness?

How long does it take for you to text back your friends? Why not use that time to do a simple act of kindness. I have this one friend on my old soccer team that was very encouraging. For example, if you made a bad pass, or made a bad shot, she was always saying, "It's okay, shake it off. You do better next time." She was determined to make February the highlight of her year. Every day, she would write on a notecard two to three sentences about a few people and give it to them. She told me her favorite part about February was watching everyone's reactions to the note cards.

You can experience kindness being shared at local places too. During the month of February, my mom was at the grocery store. When she was leaving the store, she saw an elderly woman who looked to be having a difficult time putting her groceries into her car. My mother offered to help her, at which time she accepted. The elderly woman thanked my mother multiple times and was very grateful for what she had done for her. As my mother was walking back to her car, the elderly woman saw a friend of hers. She pointed to my mom and had said, "That young lady took time to help me put my groceries in my car." The gift of kindness is always better to give than it is to receive.

It was tough trying to be nice to my sister, as she would irritate me a lot of the time, but I started doing little things for her, and we slowly started being nicer to each other.

Another heartwarming example would be how my grandfather helped a poor person with a crushed leg. This man had no money for treatment and was in the Emergency Room, but the doctors nevertheless helped him and the hospital paid for the treatment.

A couple years ago, my grandmother's driver had ditched her and never drove for her again, instead choosing to go party elsewhere. However, the driver came back after a year, looking diseased and on his deathbed. He begged for work from my grandmother, and my grandmother finally accepted. Even though the driver had ditched her, my grandmother employed him, and even went as far as admitting him to the hospital to treat him, and paying for the treatment plus a month's worth of medicine for him because he didn't have the money to do it himself. This story helped me realize what true kindness was, as the driver had backstabbed my grandmother, but when he needed help the most, my grandmother accepted him, and went further.

When my uncles were young, my granduncle did not make much money, so they could not live the leisurely life they wanted. The older uncle of the two did not mind their financial situation, but my younger uncle did. After my older uncle graduated high school, he took a part-time job to pay for his college. He noticed the misery his younger brother was going through, as he did not have fancy objects. My older uncle took the little money he earned from his part-time job for college and bought his younger brother nice shoes, and video games as well. This was amazing, as my older uncle had expected nothing in return, and he had done a truly selfless act in the process for his brother.

When I asked my grandfather about why he founded the hospital and what his goal was when he founded it, he said he did it to help patients. He had noticed that in his clinics, patients were being treated awfully slowly. He told me that "if a patient was treated in 3 days at my old clinic, I would cut that time in half in my hospital." He believed in the philosophy to "chase excellence, and success would follow." He created the hospital out of true kindness. He believed that helping patients was his obligation, and money, fame, respect all came second.

Experiences Within the team

Tatianna:

The Fabulous Five is what I like to consider Kat, Varun, Rishi, Nehali and I. Being a part of the young generation, it is hard for all of us to come together at the same time. With the obstacles we faced on the way, our group worked very well together! With the age difference between all of us, I am very surprised that we all worked great together. Being the youngest in the group, I really enjoyed connecting with everyone and getting to know them. They have made this a memory that I will never forget. "The Fabulous Five" is a group filled with young leaders that will one day use their leadership skills to help others. I'm so grateful I had the experience to work with them and the opportunity to see them grow through the group.

Varun:

None of this would have been possible without the support from Coach Divya and the team. I have enjoyed working with them, and personally, I have learned a lot from each of them. Sometimes being the "new kid" was tough, but I was able to get along with everyone. These experiences, especially ones with the Wade Edwards Learning Lab, were vital to my growth as a leader. When I went with Nehali to get introduced to the Youth Camp, I learned a lot about planning and time management from both Coach Divya and Nehali. When I went for the second time to the Youth Camp with Rishi, he taught me how to work with kids, and what to do when they will not listen. All of these lessons are amazing and have truly impacted me in the best way possible, and there would be no other way to achieve this invaluable information.

Rishi:

It has been a pleasure working with this amazing group of people. After overcoming the obstacle of getting to know each other, we not only worked as a team but as good friends. We worked through disagreements quickly and we all felt comfortable in this new environment we created for ourselves. With Coach Divya to guide us, we were able to produce a work of inspiration for future leaders. The lessons I have learned from the group have truly improved my real world actions. Working with Catherine, Tatianna, Varun, and Nehali has been fun and memorable.

Nehali:

Working with this team was an extremely unique experience. We went from complete strangers to a close team and friends in a matter of months. Each team member brought something unique to the team. One thing that struck me throughout the process of writing this book was the complete lack of arguments within our team, unless you include Shrek. We managed to work things out in a compromise before things got out of hand, or a real disagreement started. At first it was because we were uncomfortable contradicting people we barely knew, but as we grew closer, it was because we realized that that was the only way we would accomplish things successfully. This is something that we will all be able to apply in our lives going forward and something that has helped me grow as an individual.

Catherine:

I can honestly say that in my experience with the 1/1/1 Leader Project, the best part of being involved was meeting my new friends, Nehali, Rishi, Varun and Tatianna. Without them in my life, working on this book and expanding this project with me, this process wouldn't have been nearly as much fun! Being with them creates a comfortable and friendly environment, one where all ideas are respected and valued, where you can speak your mind without fear of being shot down. This entire project has been one big act of kindness, from Nehali offering to compile our stories to Rishi entertaining us during the photoshoot, and I couldn't have asked for a better team.

While this is just a small selection of random acts of kindness, the few stories we've shared have not only made impacts in our lives but will hopefully motivate others to do the same. In a time of so much hatred and hostility, these stories of compassion have shown the positive effect that even the smallest acts of kindness can have. The 1/1/1 Leader Project requires your pledge. The mission is simple: to create a community of inspired, connected, and supportive individuals. Spread, Give, Receive.

The Team in Action!

The Team in Action!

www.ingramcontent.com/pod-product-compliance
Lightning Source LLC
Chambersburg PA
CBHW022126280326
41933CB00007B/557